What are Walls for?

Christine Butterworth

Nelson

Contents

What are walls for?

People have always made walls. Walls are made for many different reasons.

There are walls of all kinds around us.

Old city wall around Canterbury

Prison wall

Great Wall of China

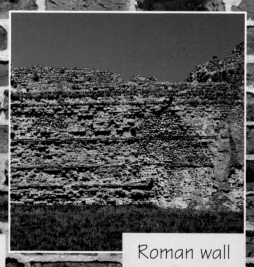

Roman wall

Walls for protection

Castles

Castles had strong walls to keep out enemy soldiers.

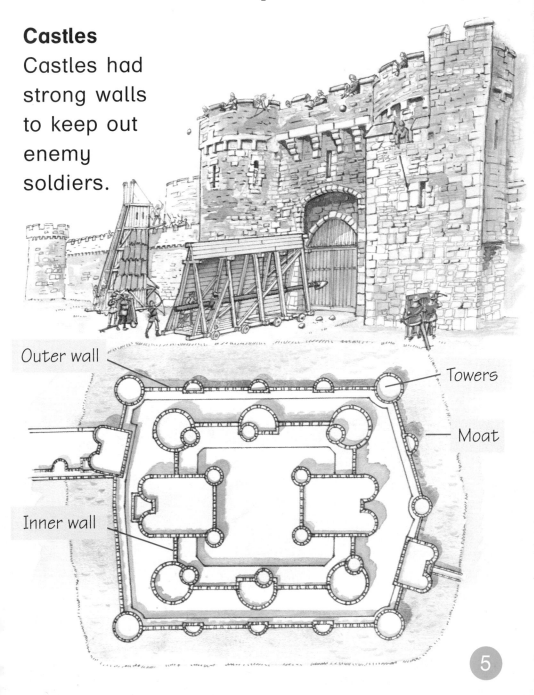

Outer wall

Towers

Moat

Inner wall

Towns

Many old towns have walls around them. They were built to keep the town safe from attack.

This wall was built in the 13th century.

Wall around Conwy, North Wales

Prisons

Prisons have high, strong walls. These walls are to stop the prisoners from escaping.

Entrance to Wormwood Scrubs prison, London

Walls for dividing

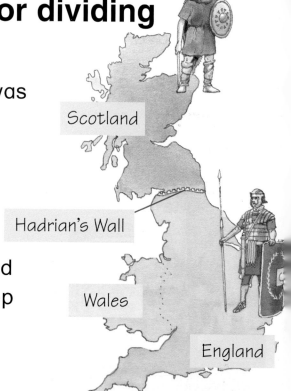

Hadrian's Wall

In 122 AD, England was part of the Roman Empire, but Scotland was not. So, the Emperor Hadrian ordered a wall to be built to divide England from Scotland, to keep Scottish tribes out.

Scotland

Hadrian's Wall

Wales

England

Part of Hadrian's Wall

Facts about Hadrian's Wall

Built:	by the Romans
Date:	about 122 AD
Materials:	rock and earth
Length:	130 km
Height:	four and a half metres

Great Wall of China

The Great Wall of China is 6,400 km long. It was built to keep the people safe from tribes that attacked them from the north.

The first part of the wall was made two thousand years ago. The last parts of the wall were built four hundred years ago.

Now, many tourists visit the wall.

The Great Wall is the only man-made thing on Earth that can be seen from space.

The Great Wall is the orange line running from top to bottom

Facts about the Great Wall of China

Built:	to keep the people safe from attack
Date:	started in 400 BC
Materials:	first mud, later stone
Length:	6,400 km
Height:	fifteen metres

The Berlin Wall

The city of Berlin was cut in two.
The Berlin Wall was built in 1961.
It was built so that people from East Berlin
could not go into West Berlin.

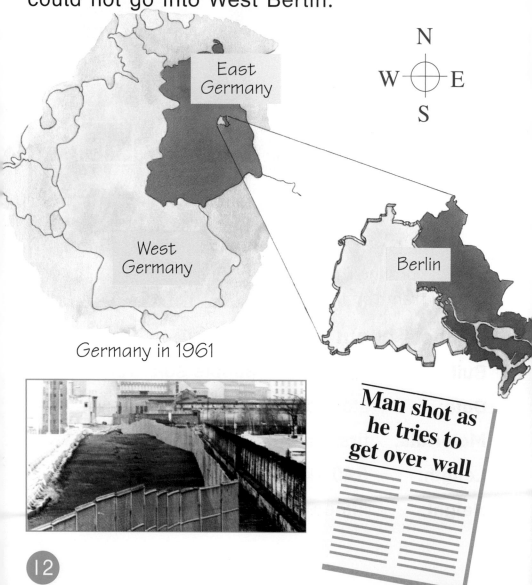

East Germany

West Germany

Germany in 1961

Berlin

N
W E
S

Man shot as he tries to get over wall

The Berlin Wall
came down on
9th November 1989.
On 1st July, 1990
East and West
Germany were
united.

Facts about the Berlin Wall

Built for: to stop people from East Berlin
                 going to West Berlin

Date: 1961

Materials: concrete, topped with barbed wire

Length: 166 km

Height: four metres

Walls for support

Houses

Walls in houses support the ceiling and keep the roof up.

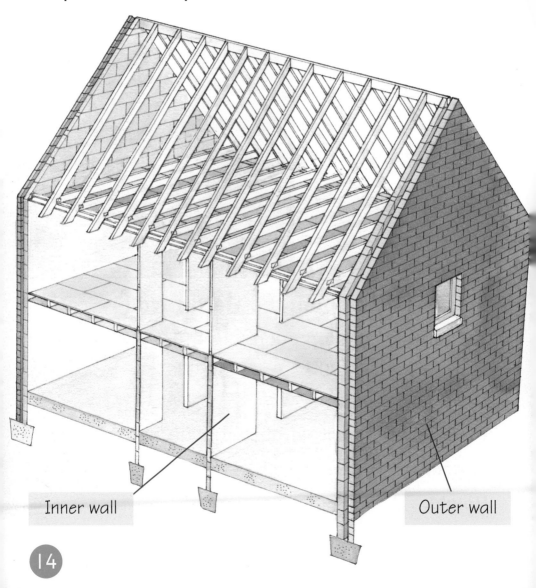

Inner wall

Outer wall

Skyscrapers

Skyscrapers need strong walls to support their many floors.

Some skyscraper walls are made of steel and glass.

Glossary

barbed wire – wire with sharp spikes

empire – a group of countries under the same ruler

emperor – the ruler of an empire

protection – keeping something safe

skyscraper – a modern building that is very tall

tourist – a person who travels to find out about things and to have fun